Aspirational Goals

Eric Scott Grand

Title: Aspirational Goals

Author: Eric Scott Grand

First Published by Manda Publishers in 2023

ISBN: 979-8-218-44554-6

Price in INR: 699/-

House of Publishing

An imprint of Manda Publishers

www.mandapublishers.com

publishat.hop@gmail.com

+91 9999190496

Cover Design: Garima

Typography: Charchit

Distributed by:

Amazon, Flipkart, Manda Publishers etc.

Printer:

Thomson press

New Delhi

About the Author:

Name - Eric Scott Grand

I have been writing poetry since 1991

I have attended convention symposiums on poetry

recorded poetry to music made into a song

attended workshops currently have two other

publications in a series of poetry

collections titled paradise on earth with words

collection 1 oceanic and paradise on earth with

words collection 2 social society now available for purchase on amazon website and Barnes and Noble website.

Contents

Aspirational goals

It's to do what's required to have more in some form

they're

aspirational goals that

can be written on a list to later finish if

there's a situation to mention that meets your

expectations to grow they're

aspirational goals

that's prepared before it's shared that makes

it a habit to put into practice

till their met they're

aspirational goals

it's a point to reach

to complete that's fulfill

to learn a skill to be done

when your young to accomplish
when you're old they're

aspirational goals

that's set to get what's expect
if planned correct
not leave in woe
they're
aspirational goals
that put in the effort that involves dedication,
not to be a failure instead excel

do well

that they earn they're aspirational goals
it's to do for future use

that almost seems impossible they're

aspirational goals

that gives some relief after

to have some freedom

to have more control they're

aspirational goals

that's announce

when it's known for sure they're

aspirational goals.

Built for success

Over achievers ready to compete amongst
the best are built for success when they enter
contests they set out to not do the worst only

be first that what they set out to accomplish
they're built for success who are ambitious
confident in their decisions; they put

into use they practice they're

built for success

goal minded individuals who tackle
what they can manage that's a challenge
to make progress are built for success that's

character to be
better is put to the test they're
built for success they
do what they say that don't

like to wait they

come prepared they're built for success

positive people who find ways to improve
at their own expense they're built for success that
have their pride to prosper thrive to perceive in
their career they invent they're built
for success the time effort they put shows,

in the good results they get they're

built for success.

Great

To be great is to set the record straight not sit wait

caught up with age to be great isn't to make the

same mistake for time not to decide your fate to be great

to be great experiences turnout your way

throughout the
day that

may have some help to be safe

to give aid to be

great

that goes lengths to reach a certain state

to get to a
designated place to

be great

to be great is brought up to speed

to arrive without being late to

be great does whatever at stake

as long as it benefits to get ahead

for goodness sake to

be great

Meant for greatness

It's to go the extra stretch to be the best

have high expectations when you're meant for greatness

it's

to make a commitment have

discipline to

use your common sense to

strive for excellence when you're meant for

greatness to

go to an extreme to achieve an impossibility

to succeed

in excess when you're meant for greatness

it's to go to a distance that's a long extent

reach success when you're meant for greatness to

pursue what's hard to imagine

that takes several years to accomplish

that's a long process to progress

when

you're meant for greatness to

have dedication without limitations

deal with mistakes have

patience to endure much

not rewarded enough

not get much credit for all your effort gain

when you're meant for greatness

it's to go a length that makes wait to present it

that involves to participate

when you're meant for

greatness when

you're able to be at a point in your career

what could not be repeat to get to

a pinnacle of your profession

when you're

meant for greatness to

go beyond what never has been done

with the assistance of no one to guide

advise that you're only able to comprehend

when you're meant for greatness.

Optimism

It makes conditions for improvement to increase not be

disappointing later that isn't skepticism it's

optimism that reassures any doubt that may

emerge without

cynicism it's optimism that

situations

are inclined to side what is like without

negativism it's optimism

it's susceptible to boost morale that raises

the spirit it's optimism when

it changes your attitude your

mood is good not

have antagonism it's optimism that's

for enhancement not pessimism it's optimism

it changes behavior prior to a competition won

it's optimism that makes rally up gather around prepare

for a comeback to win it's

optimism that can make

be triumphant

after going through a slump turnout later

to be rank number one it's optimism.

Potential

Has capabilities to achieve

what it needs to complete that's

influential has potential

That

demonstrates what it does is for a good cause that's

professional has potential that can function

at an optimal level has potential

shows that can perform

to receive be in a position to have a better status

that's not accidental has potential

proves that it can do what's difficult

without question

to later decide you're able to

confide with matters

that are confidential has potential that's entrusted

with duties to advance that their actions

are credible has potential

convinces that it could do what seems impossible

under pressure that's stressful has potential that's

put in a position under their directions

to make

corrections to be successful has potential that it

turns out exceptional that's memorable is

commendable has potential.

Raised for excellence

When nurtured developed in an astute household

told what you're to do is meant to be important

when you're raised for excellence

you're placed in a category

with like

minded individuals that are special that

pull off feats that succeed

that been mastered over the

years

that gives confidence when you're raised for excellence

you're

made aware what done now at

an

early stage in life will pay off later

then it will

make sense when you're

raised for

excellence

when you're let known when grown
you'll
accomplish much that's good for ordinance
when
you're raised for excellence you're
advised to do your best
you're reminded don't settle for
anything less
when you're raised for excellence
you're
able to learn more on your own
follow your advice that comes from within
that guides that
involves phases stages
to take appropriate steps when you're raised
for excellence

when realized you're expected more
of from the start it can be hard

when you're raised

for excellence you're to do what has to be done

at your own expense when you're raised

for excellence then

you're faced with obstacles

that makes responsible with a challenge

that has to be manage with experience

when you're raised for excellence.

Scholarships

Pays your way to educate

in any need to buy supplies

with not much to spend are scholarships that

must meet a

requirement to acquire them

are scholarships their earned on how well

you've learn that shows on exam scores that

are rewards for good merits are scholarships

finances

expenses for academics are scholarships

covers costs to shop what's required to have

are

scholarships that come in forms to apply

to see if qualified if can get are scholarships

gives credit where credit is due to students

who show good aptitude

for their high marks

are scholarships it helps for your future

they

fund are scholarships that assists with tools

like reading materials to be more intelligent

are scholarships.

Scholastic achievements

Abiding guidelines required to qualify for enrollment

Meant

to complete are scholastic

achievements if

the prerequisite is met that's worth it

look forward to set goals advance in a class that

a

grade is received are scholastic achievements followed

rules with good aptitude with examination

to determine their qualification that they're

in good

standards to believe are scholastic achievements

On a right path to study then receive

a degree

are scholastic achievements then applied what's learn

to live normal that's convenient

are scholastic achievements that come earning a certificate

to get paid decent are scholastic achievements

complied

with regulations to get an education

then earned is a diploma that adds up to credentials

that succeeds are scholastic achievements

that's easier to find employment in a career

are scholastic achievements that's practical ethical

for academics to earn money

with are scholastic achievements.

Smart

Found a way to persuade that can make change
that's explained that will not cause to be alarm is smart
that knows

how to speak with reason to be treated equally
emotionally
to not be harsh is smart learned
how to use words in a format that's
proper is smart

thought
out on its own how to come up with a solution
with no confusion to cause is smart came
up with a plan to make
understand
that is not hard is smart
what's
difficult to imagine that takes patience
to get done is smart

completed what needed to be

achieve with no problem is smart that is

clever to do what it does is smart that has

the know how to finish what it starts is smart

The finer luxury experiences in life

You're attended to every need that gets done with speed

you're

given special attention to get what's requested

that

it turns out right are the finer

luxury experiences

in life

preparations are made in advance to come out

like it's supposed to be plan there's

always ways to see improvements

to make without time waste there's

pursuits to pursue in order to do good

that makes places to go people to see to

keep busy to stay alive are the finer luxury experiences

in life

there's more to share in order to give

to live there's many rewards that's splurge

to buy are the finer luxury experiences in life

you're

catered to what's to your liking

that's included with power privilege prestige

however, it's decided are the finer luxury

experiences in life there's opportunities to succeed

there are ways to barter with reimbursements

to supplement income, get paid are the finer luxury

experiences in life there's time to process ways to help

for others to do well that your treated equally quickly to

prosper thrive are the finer luxury experiences in life

your

served to whatever desired handled fast

you're thought of first reminded to do

than just get by are the finer luxury experiences in life

arrangements

are put into action prior to get

what's expected available are chance for

enhancements with unlimited amount of resources

at your disposal to try are the finer luxury experiences

in life when reach this point your

entitled to have your own style

share personal beliefs to be unique

give advice are the finer luxury experiences in life.

Wealth

Money hungry the need for greed to exceed

beyond your wildest dreams it puts in charge the

payoff is large to maintain it is hard with

wealth it is exclusive to the lucrative

a big expense that draws great interest anything

is possible with wealth when your

profitable you're in control

when

there's cash flow a financial gain

well into the millions a melting pot valued a lot Swiss

bank accounts checks don't bounce

stocks bonds credit funds every dollar can count

with wealth eager for currency to maximize

capitalize to reinvent yourself with wealth items

that didn't seemed worth are purchased to improve

your mood that helps with wealth that ensures your

situation that there could be no doubts with

wealth

anxious for bullion to invest in that's sufficient

it's substantial with wealth personal growth can soar

to be financially secure with wealth that has to be

handled

managed for it to

be carefully dealt with wealth

www.ingramcontent.com/pod-product-compliance
Lightning Source LLC
Chambersburg PA
CBHW071227140726
47996CB00004B/1509